DODD, MEAD WONDERS BOOKS include WONDERS OF:

CATTLE. Scuro
CORALS AND CORAL REEFS. Jacobson and Franz
CROWS. Blassingame
DONKEYS. Lavine and Scuro
DRAFT HORSES. Lavine and Casey
DUST. McFall
EAGLE WORLD. Lavine
EGRETS, BITTERNS, AND HERONS. Blassingame
ELEPHANTS. Lavine and Scuro
FLIGHTLESS BIRDS. Lavine
FROGS AND TOADS. Blassingame
GEESE AND SWANS. Fegely
GOATS. Lavine and Scuro
HIPPOS. Lavine
LIONS. Schaller
MARSUPIALS. Lavine
MICE. Lavine
MULES. Lavine and Scuro
PEACOCKS. Lavine
PIGS. Lavine and Scuro
PONIES. Lavine and Casey
RACCOONS. Blassingame
RATTLESNAKES. Chace
RHINOS. Lavine
SEA HORSES. Brown
SEALS AND SEA LIONS. Brown
SHARKS. Blassingame
SHEEP. Lavine and Scuro
SNAILS AND SLUGS. Jacobson and Franz
SPONGES. Jacobson and Pang
TURKEYS. Lavine and Scuro
TURTLE WORLD. Blassingame
WILD DUCKS. Fegely
WOODCHUCKS. Lavine
WORLD OF BEARS. Bailey
WORLD OF HORSES. Lavine and Casey
ZEBRAS. Scuro

1983 SEA WORLD OF FLORIDA

WONDERS OF
SHARKS

Wyatt Blassingame

Illustrated with photographs

Dodd, Mead & Company New York

To Pearl McCoy—with thanks, and love

Distributed in Canada by
McClelland and Stewart Limited, Toronto
Manufactured in the United States of America

1 2 3 4 5 6 7 8 9 10

Library of Congress Cataloging in Publication Data

Blassingame, Wyatt.
Wonders of sharks.

Includes index.
Summary: Describes the physical characteristics, habits, and natural environment of various species of sharks.
1. Sharks—Juvenile literature. [1. Sharks]
I. Title.
QL638.9.B53 1984 597'.31 84-10097
ISBN 0-396-08463-X

Frontispiece: *A sand tiger shark*

CONTENTS

1983 SEA WORLD OF FLORIDA

Sharks are found in all the oceans of the world, but especially in warm and temperate waters. This is a sandbar shark, sometimes called a brown shark.

1. *SHARK!*

A newspaper once tried to learn what word in the English language had the most frightening effect on people. Reporters stopped men and women on the street to ask their reaction to words like *murder, rape, starvation, suicide.*

And the word that the majority of people found most terrifying was *Shark!*

Even the word has an ugly sound. It comes from the German *schurke,* which means a villain or a greedy parasite that feeds on other life. One whole group of sharks is named the requiem sharks, and a requiem is a song for the dead.

Sharks are by no means rare. They are found in all the oceans, but especially in warm and temperate waters. In summer some sharks migrate in huge schools as far north as Newfoundland, then south again in winter. Some species even go into freshwater and have been found miles up the Mississippi River. Yet many of the people who are most frightened by the mere

U. S. NAVY

Shark expert Dr. David Baldridge says, "Sharks don't swim, they fly." By this he means that sharks move through the water much as airplanes move through the air. To illustrate, he uses these two photographs: head views of a shark and a modern commercial plane.

U. S. NAVY

thought of a shark have never seen one. Chances are they never will, unless it is in an aquarium or mounted on a wall.

The truth is that three times as many persons are killed by beestings each year in the United States alone as are killed by sharks in all the waters of the world.

More persons are hit by lightning than are bitten by sharks.

Why then does the word "shark" flash such horrible pictures across the imagination of so many persons?

Perhaps it is because most people know very little about sharks. In the absence of knowledge the imagination is free to work overtime. For air-breathing human beings the world beneath the sea is foreign, strange, often terrifying. Even the thought of putting one's face beneath the surface frightens many children, and some adults. So it has always been easy to fear the ghostly creatures of the sea that we know so little about. And the most frightening of those creatures always has been the mysterious, terrifying, but strangely beautiful shark.

It was not until the middle of the twentieth century that scientists began to study sharks seriously. During World War II there were horrifying stories of ships being sunk, planes shot down at sea, and their crews devoured by sharks. Most of these stories were wildly exaggerated, but certainly they affected the morale of sailors and airmen who ran these risks. So the government asked scientists to learn how shark attacks might be prevented. To do this the scientists had first to learn the true nature of sharks.

These studies are still going on. And the shark has proved to be a fascinating creature well worth learning about.

2. *WHAT IS A SHARK?*

Scientifically sharks belong to a group of fishes called elasmobranchs. This group also includes stingrays, giant manta rays, and their other ray and skate relatives. But rays and sharks are not classed together because they look alike. Most sharks are long, slender, tube-shaped from nose to tail. Most rays are pancake-flat with whiplike tails. But all the elasmobranchs, unlike other fish, have skeletons made of cartilage rather than bone. This is a strong, fibrous material. It makes up the harder parts of the human ear and nose. It is not as hard as bone, but is more elastic.

Most fish have only a single pair of gill slits. Sharks and rays have several. With rays, most of these are under the head. With sharks, they are on the sides of the head.

Most fish have a swim bladder—a sort of air-filled balloon which helps keep them afloat. Sharks do not.

Also the shark's scales are actually tiny, hard teeth. One

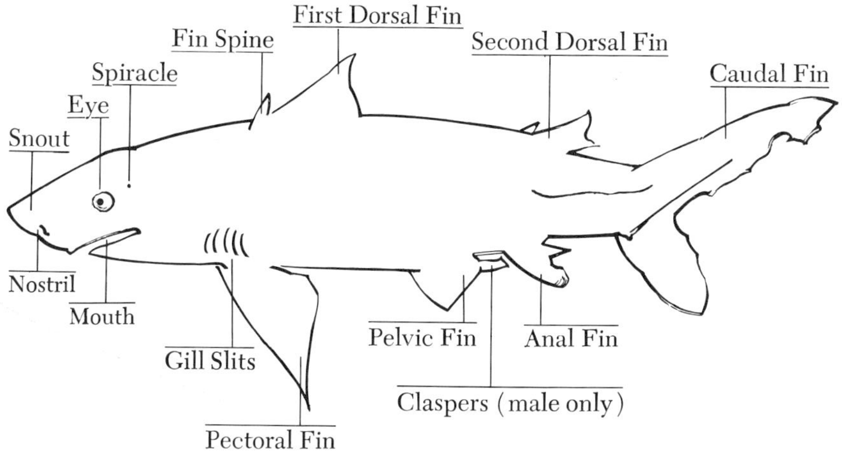

PEARL MC COY

Diagram of a shark

naturalist wrote that the scales of most fish compare to those of a shark like the tinfoil wrapper on chewing gum compares to the armor of a tank.

So, scientifically, a shark is a fish with a skeleton of cartilage, five to seven pairs of gill slits on the sides of its head, no swim bladder, and scales made of the same material as its teeth. There are other points that define a shark, but these are the main ones.

There are, however, an amazing number and variety of fish that fit into the scientific family of sharks. There are, indeed, about 350 species—nobody knows exactly. There are whale sharks that may grow to forty feet long and weigh over twenty-six thousand pounds. There are rare Pacific Ocean sharks that, fully grown, are about six inches long. There are angel sharks—called angels because their pectoral fins have grown long and wide to look like wings. The hammerhead shark has a head like a hammer, and the saw shark has a snout like a saw.

In fact, there are so many species of sharks that almost anything said about them in general will have some exceptions.

ROBERT PRESNAL, BEACH CAMERA

This is a close-up photograph of the teeth of a great hammerhead shark. It shows how the teeth grow in rows, coming out of the jaw in a sort of endless belt.

The Sharks' Teeth

Because the shark's skeleton is made of cartilage rather than bone, it rarely turned into fossils. And so paleontologists, the scientists who study the forms of life from prehistoric times, have comparatively few shark skeletons to learn from. On the other hand they do have sharks' teeth. A vast amount of them!

It is the teeth that have made sharks so famous. Or infamous. Many people picture a shark as one huge mouthful of long, gleaming, triangular teeth. And many sharks do have such teeth. However, some bottom-feeding sharks, which eat things like crabs and clams, have teeth meant more for grinding their food than for tearing it to bits. Naturalists can often tell one species of shark from another by the shape of the teeth. But whatever the species, the teeth are unusual.

If human beings had teeth like sharks there would be little

need for dentists. A human being has two sets of teeth: baby teeth that eventually fall out, and one other set that may, or may not, last the rest of your life.

A shark has many sets at the same time, usually five. And it keeps right on growing new ones. The front set of teeth is the largest. This is the set that does most of the work in ripping or grinding the food. A few species use more than one set of teeth at a time in feeding, but in most it is the front set that does the work. Back of it is another smaller set of teeth. And behind that still another. And another. Smaller and smaller. The small upper teeth lie almost flat against the roof of the shark's mouth, the lower teeth back against the jaw.

As the front set of teeth wears down, it falls out. What had been the second set moves into first place, the third set into

WILLIAM M. STEPHENS

A tiger shark tooth has a distinctive shape. This tooth is from a fourteen-foot specimen, and it is sharp enough to shave with.

CAPTAIN CLYDE FORE

The sand tiger shark can be identified by its long, narrow, smooth-edged teeth. At the corners of the mouth, the teeth are very small and very numerous.

second. And so on. A new set begins to form where the smallest set had been. It is very much like an endless belt.

As a young shark grows, its head needs more teeth. One scientist working with lemon sharks learned that the young lose a set of teeth about every seven or eight days. The whole set might not fall out at exactly the same time, but on the whole the rows of teeth move forward together.

With full-grown adult sharks the loss of teeth is slower, but exactly how slow no one has yet been able to learn. An adult probably gets between seven to twelve sets a year.

It is from these plentiful teeth, along with some other fossils, that scientists have been able to learn about the ancestors of today's sharks.

3. *SHARK EVOLUTION*

The first sharks of which we have any knowledge were swimming in the warm oceans of the world some 400 million years ago. Scientists now call them cladodonts, a name they get from the shape of their teeth. These had two and sometimes more points, which were meant for tearing their food. So probably they were predators, like most of their relatives today. Many, however, seem to have been comparatively small, probably no more than three feet long. While they ate small fish, they were in turn eaten by larger ones.

About 225 million years ago the last of the cladodonts disappeared. By then, however, there were many new species of sharks. Some of these ruled the oceans as completely as the great white shark does today. In fact, one of them had teeth as big as seven inches long. Scientists figure that as a rule one inch of shark tooth equals ten feet of body length in adult sharks. That means some of these sharks must have been seventy feet

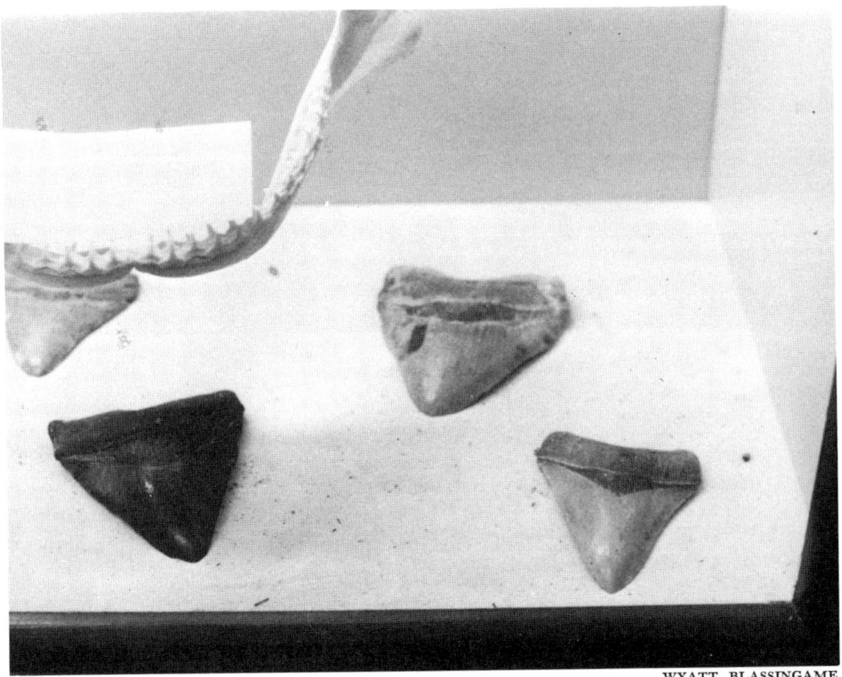

WYATT BLASSINGAME

These are the teeth of prehistoric sharks worn smooth by thousands of years of being rolled by currents along the ocean bottom. The largest is six inches long.

long—more than three times the length of the biggest great white shark ever positively identified.

What brought an end to these monsters is unknown. We do know that by the end of what scientists call the Cretaceous period, about 135 to 165 million years ago, there were sharks just like the ones we have today. And like today's sharks they shed their teeth in large numbers. People find them today. Some of the places they are found tell a great deal about how our earth has changed from time to time.

On the flat plains of Kansas, where in late summer the wheat fields lie level and golden from one horizon to the other, farmers' plows sometimes turn up shark teeth.

Shark teeth are embedded in the walls of the Grand Canyon, along with the dried remains of sponges.

In the ancient Appalachian mountains, in the Andes, in the Himalayas, "the rooftop of the world," there are shark teeth.

Near Baltimore, Maryland, what was once ocean floor is now rolling hill country. Here Dr. Eugenie Clark, one of the world authorities on sharks, sometimes hunts for shark teeth by climbing cliffs, digging into them with hammers. On the other hand, near Englewood, Florida, the land is sinking. The sea's ancient settlement is being washed away by the tides. Here almost every wave uncovers a scattering of shark teeth. Currents moving up and down the coast add to the supply. Here a person strolling the beach can often pick them up by the dozen.

4. *HOW A SHARK FINDS ITS FOOD*

Hunting its food in the vast open sea, the shark has three senses on which it chiefly relies. These are smell, sight, and the vibration of the water—the shark's "hearing." Of these, the sense of smell is usually thought to be the most important. Although the shark's brain is small for the size of its body—some persons believe the shark's brain does not even record the sense of pain—a very large part of that brain is given to the sense of smell. Some scientists refer to the shark as a "swimming nose."

The shark's nostrils are on the underside of its snout, just ahead of the mouth. But they have no connection with the mouth. In fact, they have nothing to do with breathing. They are for smelling only, and they do an excellent job. Each nostril is a kind of cup filled with olfactory cells, the cells that sense odors. As the shark moves, or even when it lies still, water constantly flows in and out of each nostril, constantly bathing the olfactory cells.

Dr. Perry Gilbert has studied sharks for over thirty years. In

MOTE MARINE LABORATORY

Dr. Perry Gilbert studying a tiger shark at the Mote Marine Laboratory.

one experiment he learned that where a strong sea current is flowing, sharks could detect the odor of blood more than a quarter of a mile away. Also a very small bit of tuna—one of the shark's favorite foods—was smelled by sharks seventy-five feet away. At that distance there was about one part of tuna juice to every 1.5 million parts of water!

"Hearing"

The hunting shark has another sense to rely on that is almost as keen as its sense of smell. This is called the lateralis system.

WILLIAM M. STEPHENS

Dr. Donald Nelson, an expert on the "hearing" of sharks, performs a conditioning experiment to determine how well this small lemon shark discriminates between sounds of different frequencies. The shark "hears" by the reaction of its lateralis system to vibrations in the water.

It consists of very fine canals, just beneath the skin, that run along each side of the shark from tail to head, and across the head. These canals are filled with a watery fluid. Scattered along the canals are small pores that open to the surface.

Any noise or motion in water causes a vibration. When that vibration strikes the open pores of the lateralis system, a message is sent to the shark's brain just as if the shark had been touched by some solid object. This helps the shark find its prey at night or in murky water where it cannot see.

Morever, the shark can tell the vibrations made by a healthy fish that would be hard to capture from those of an injured one. William Beebe, the famous naturalist, proved this in the Galápagos Islands. Looking down through clear water he saw a number of sharks. Small fish swam all around them, unnoticed.

Beebe let down a hook and caught one of the small fish. It began to struggle—and instantly the sharks whirled toward it, whether or not they had been looking in that direction. He repeated the experiment over and over, always with the same result.

During World War II it was learned that whenever a ship was sunk by torpedoes, sharks came from long distances to investigate. But exactly how sensitive the lateralis system is no one yet knows. This will require some imaginative research by future scientists.

Other fish also have similar systems, but because the shark sometimes attacks human beings, more research has been done on it than on other species.

The Eyes

The shark has another aid in finding its prey—its eyes. For a long while it was believed that the shark's eyesight was very poor. But actually the shark sees better than most people had believed. In fact, it is unusually sensitive to light. Hunting at

At the University of Miami's Rosenstiel School of Marine and Atmospheric Science, classical conditioning techniques are used to test the vision of sharks. Note the vertical slit pupil characteristic of the lemon shark.

J. GALINDO

night or in the depths of the ocean it needs to be. And its eyes have a special aid, one it shares with cats and some other night-prowling animals. This is something called the *tapetum lucidum.* It is a mirrorlike layer in the back of the eye: Light comes through the eye and is reflected back again. In this way the part of the eye sensitive to light is stimulated twice.

Usually, then, the hungry shark will first locate its prey by either smell or by vibrations in the water. As it draws closer, the shark swings its head from side to side, picking up the smell first in one nostril, then the other.

As it draws still closer, its eyes take over. The exact distance is largely determined by the amount of light and the clarity of the water. But certainly sharks use their eyes in the final moments of attack.

The Ampullae of Lorenzini

Human beings may use sight and smell, and even vibrations of the air, in hunting. But the sharks have one sense that is foreign to the human body—at least in the everyday meaning. Every living animal gives off a small field of electricity. Dr. Eugenie Clark has found that the shark is more sensitive to this electrical field than any animal yet studied. Many sharks like to feed on their relatives, the stingrays. And stingrays often lie buried in the sand, invisible, motionless. But the cruising shark can sense the electric field of the stingray, nose it out of the sand, and eat it.

The shark does this by means of something called the ampullae of Lorenzini. The ampullae are the swollen parts of canals that lie just under the skin of the shark's head and open to the surface. Lorenzini is the scientist who discovered them. The ampullae of Lorenzini is something very much like the shark's lateralis system, but it is confined to the shark's head. It not only helps the shark find food, but it acts as a kind of built-in compass. With it some species navigate the trackless wastes of the ocean, knowing exactly where they are at all times.

This ampullae of Lorenzini may have still another use. Sharks often rub their heads against objects before biting them, or before turning away without biting. Some naturalists believe that with this bumping the shark uses the ampullae of Lorenzini to taste, or in some other way determine whether or not the object is edible.

5. *HOW SHARKS REPRODUCE*

Some sharks are oviparous. Some are ovoviviparous. And some are viviparous.

Those are fancy words, but the meanings are simple—if anything about reproduction can be called simple.

All sharks have internal fertilization. The male shark has *claspers* that lie just back of the pelvic fins. Through these the male sperm is passed into the female's body to fertilize the eggs. But how the eggs develop varies with the different species. And this is where the fancy words come in.

The oviparous species of sharks lay eggs, much as birds or hens lay eggs, except that shark eggs have a different shape and texture. The outside is very tough and leathery. With some species it is an almost flat rectangle, with others it is screw-shaped. The rectangular eggs have long tendrils at the corners. These tie themselves to rocks or plants on the bottom of the sea. The screw-shaped eggs bore into the bottom. Inside each egg, no matter its shape, is a yolk on which the developing baby feeds until finally, like a chicken, it is ready to break free. But unlike the baby chick or bird, the baby shark is fully developed and able to look after itself. Oviparous mother sharks never see their young. Or if they do, they are quite likely to eat them, because the oviparous young are comparatively small. The whale shark, which may grow to forty feet, has an egg about fourteen inches long. But no matter its size, most baby sharks are born with a mouth full of teeth, able to swim, and ready to feed on just about anything smaller than it is.

Viviparous sharks are born in much the same way as human beings and other mammals. The baby develops inside the female and is fed through the placenta, a part of the mother's body. With some species of sharks this period of development may take almost two years—as long or longer than with elephants. With others it is much shorter. The number of young, called pups, will also vary. With most species the number is somewhere between two and twenty, but it may be as many as a hundred.

Baby viviparous sharks, like their oviparous relatives, are born fully developed and ready to look after themselves. In some species, such as the great white shark, the baby may be over four feet long. In fact, the baby shark is armed for defense even before birth. Stewart Springer, who has studied sharks for many years, was once examining a female that had been caught by fishermen and hauled onto a dock in the Florida Keys. Springer opened the shark's belly and found a half dozen living, unborn babies. When he reached to touch one, it slashed his finger to the bone. "And I just wanted to put it back in the water," Springer said later.

It is lucky, from the baby shark's point of view, that it is born able to look after itself. If it were to hang around the mother, she would eat it. Sharks do not hesitate to feed on one another

WILLIAM M. STEPHENS

Dr. Eugenie Clark (right) is known for her scientific studies of shark behavior. Here, she and her assistant, Oley Farver (left), are removing young brown sharks from the uterus of a female shark that died while being transported to the lab for studies. At center is one of the Vanderbilts, patrons of the Cape Haze Marine Laboratory (now Mote Marine Laboratory).

where possible. However, some naturalists believe that the female thresher shark loses her appetite at the time of birth. By the time she recovers it, the babies are long gone.

On the other hand, many naturalists believe the female thresher is as likely to gobble up her own young as any other shark.

As the name ovoviviparous suggests, these sharks have something in common with both the oviparous and the viviparous species. Ovoviviparous babies develop inside the mother's body, but they are not fed by a placenta. Instead, each baby, and there may be twenty or more, starts as an ordinary egg in a shell. But unlike the oviparous sharks, the eggs hatch while still inside the mother. Each newly hatched baby then feeds on any unfertilized eggs it can find—and on any smaller brothers and sisters. Usually only one baby out of a litter survives to be born. It is, like its other relatives, fully able to look after itself.

6. THE STUDY OF SHARKS

Sharks may be captured in nets or on hook and line. But to study a live shark under laboratory conditions it must be moved from the open sea to the aquarium. And this is not always easy.

Any large fish lifted from the water into the air may suffer serious injury. The fish's natural home is in water, and water helps support its internal organs. This is particularly true of sharks where the skeleton is made of cartilage, much less rigid than bone. Merely lifting a large shark by its tail will, usually, fatally injure it. Some of its internal organs may simply spill from its mouth.

Its death, however, will not be quick. And here is one of the strangest things about sharks. A shark may be caught by hook and line, fight until it is exhausted, be hauled onto a dock and left for hours, apparently dead. Then someone will try to push it into the water and it may whirl and bite. Fishing boats have often caught sharks, slit them wide open, and thrown them

The shark normally spends its life lying horizontally, much of its intestinal weight supported by the surrounding water. So it does not need muscular support for its stomach. Lifted out of the water, head down, its stomach may spill out of its mouth, as has happened with this shark.

CAPTAIN CLYDE FORE

back overboard. And the sharks will not only swim for awhile but often turn and begin to feed on their own entrails.

But if a shark is to be kept alive in captivity, it needs careful handling. It may be towed slowly back to the holding pen or aquarium where it is to be kept. Even so, a shark handled in this way may die. So now specially built boats are often used. Some have a big live well opening through the stern of the boat. The hooked and exhausted shark may be led into this without ever being lifted from the water.

WILLIAM M. STEPHENS

Dr. Eugenie Clark and Oley Farver pull a bull shark into the boat for carrying live specimens.

CAPTAIN CLYDE FORE

This shark is being carried in a stretcher from one part of the marine laboratory to another.

If the shark boat does not have a live well that opens directly into the water, the shark must be lifted aboard. To do this the hooked shark is brought close to the boat. A canvas sling is carefully slipped around it. The shark is hoisted from the water like a man on a stretcher, and lowered into the live well. In the live well water flows constantly over the shark's gills to keep it breathing.

Even with the most careful handling the shark may be injured or be so exhausted that in the aquarium it makes no attempt to swim. For many species of sharks this would mean death. Sharks, like other fish, breathe by taking oxygen out of the water with their gills. But to do this many species of sharks have to keep moving in order to keep the water flowing across the gill slits. Some species, such as the nurse shark, can lie still

WYATT BLASSINGAME

All sharks must swim in order to stay afloat, but not all must swim in order to breathe. These two are resting peacefully on the bottom of the Mote Marine Laboratory aquarium. To breathe, the lemon shark (above) not only moves its gills, but constantly opens and closes its mouth. The nurse shark (below) simply waves its gills, its mouth shut.

WYATT BLASSINGAME

1983 SEA WORLD OF FLORIDA

When a shark is brought into an aquarium from the open sea, it may be too tired to swim. Left alone, it would sink and drown, since it needs to keep water passing over its gills in order to breathe. Here a brown shark is being walked, until it has rested enough to swim on its own.

and breathe by fanning the gills to bring freshwater across them. But other species must move constantly in order to breathe. If such a shark is too tired to swim when brought to an aquarium, it must be "walked" to keep it alive. To do this handlers push the shark slowly forward so that freshwater flows constantly across its gills.

Though not all sharks must swim all the time in order to breathe, *all* of them must swim *all* the time in order to stay afloat. Remember that the shark has no swim bladder. So it is heavier than the water around it. If it does not swim, it sinks. Dr. Perry Gilbert studied this at the Mote Marine Laboratory in Sarasota, Florida.

It has been known for some time that sharks can be tranquil-

Sharks can be tranquilized by injection or spraying their gills with certain chemicals. This eleven-foot tiger shark has been tranquilized in order to be carefully examined. Notice that only the head and tail have been lifted clear of the water, so that most of its internal organs are still supported by water.

OCEAN WORLD, INC.

Dr. David Baldridge at the "racetrack" tank of the Mote Marine Laboratory. Here he is learning the underwater weight of a shark.

CAPTAIN CLYDE FORE

ized by injections or by spraying a chemical called MS-222 on the gills. Dr. David Baldridge did this to a large tiger shark at the Mote Marine Laboratory. Then it was lifted carefully on a stretcher, so as not to injure it, and weighed. In the air the shark weighed 1,015 pounds.

The shark was put back in the water. Here the shark was reweighed, using a complicated but precise method Baldridge had invented. In the water the shark weighed 7.3 pounds.

Any other animal that weighed a thousand pounds in the open air would weigh a lot more than seven pounds in the water. Why did the shark weigh so little?

The answer is the shark's liver. All sharks have extremely large livers. In some species the liver will make up almost 25 percent of its total weight. And this liver creates a large amount of oil that is lighter than water.

And here is another strange thing about sharks: The more the shark eats, the less it may weigh! The liver of a well-fed shark manufactures a lot of oil. The oil is lighter than the water around the shark. In the water a lean and hungry shark weighs more than a fat, well-fed one.

The newly captured shark may not start to eat for several days, or even weeks. In fact, one ten-foot tiger shark at the Cape Haze Laboratory did not start to eat for five months. Once it does start to feed, a nine- or ten-foot shark will need about fifteen pounds of fish a day. But if given the chance it will gulp down thirty pounds, or more. Then it will be very picky about its food for the next day or so, eating little or nothing. It is probable that in the open sea a shark may kill a fish as large or larger than itself, eat all it can possibly hold, and then go several days, or even weeks, before it feeds again.

How Sharks Eat

Except in a few species, the shark's mouth is on the underside of its long, pointed snout. Many persons believe that when a shark attacks, it must turn on its back or its side in order to bite. If the shark's mouth was like that of a human being, that might be true. In human beings the upper jaw is fixed to the skull. Only the lower jaw moves. But when a shark opens its mouth, both jaws move. The upper jaw shifts forward and up. In some species even the teeth move into a new position.

Sometimes a shark may turn on its side to attack, but usually it comes straight at the bait. It does this even if the bait is bigger than the shark. It raises its head, opens its mouth. Usually the teeth of the lower jaw strike first, then the upper jaw. At this point the shark lashes its head from side to side, ripping loose a mouthful of flesh. And, depending on the shark's size, this may be quite a mouthful.

Valerie Taylor and her husband, Ron, have spent years photographing sharks underwater. While making the movie *Blue Water, White Death* they used a dead whale to attract sharks. At first only one or two sharks appeared, then more and more until they swarmed around the whale in uncounted numbers, tearing it apart. Later Valerie Taylor wrote that the sharks went "diving into the whale, then swimming out again, huge lumps of oily flesh hanging from their maws, blood flowing from their gills. Some hung to the carcass, shuddering their way through flesh and sinew, tearing, gulping, swallowing in a continuous spasm of gluttony."

At times like this sharks may go into what is called a "feeding frenzy." A number of sharks appear to go totally insane, not so much from hunger as from a wild impulse to strike at anything in front of them. Attacking a huge bait such as the dead whale, they may slash one another. A dozen may turn on a wounded shark and devour it even while the wounded shark keeps feeding.

Such a feeding frenzy usually starts suddenly, and ends just as suddenly. Some of the bait that started the frenzy may still be uneaten. The sharks swim away from it and away from each other, disappearing in the depths.

But sharks do not need to be in a feeding frenzy to eat strange things. Sailors on a freight boat noticed a huge shark following close behind. When a sack of coal fell overboard, the shark calmly gulped it down. The sailors began to throw over other objects: newspapers, a brick wrapped in cloth, a broken alarm clock, a packing crate. The shark swallowed them all, one after another.

A fisherman on a South African beach caught a large tiger shark. When he opened its stomach he found half a crocodile, including the head, the hind leg of a sheep, three sea gulls, two

THE ISLANDER

This large grouper was attacked by sharks before the fisherman could land it. The sharks got the best part.

unopened cans of peas, and a sealed tin of cigarettes. But why sharks will sometimes swallow such things as unopened cans and broken alarm clocks, no one knows for sure.

Strange as it may seem, the contents of one shark's stomach helped to solve a murder case in Australia. This shark had been captured alive and brought to an aquarium. There it swam about for several weeks without eating anything. Then, suddenly, it vomited up the arm of a man, complete and undigested. In fact, it was in such good condition that tattoo marks on it were plainly visible. From the tattoo, police were able to identify the victim—a man who had been in trouble with known criminals and had simply disappeared. Police had suspected murder but had no proof. Now doctors could tell by the condition of the arm that it had been removed from the body not by a shark, but by a knife. The man had been murdered, dismembered, and the parts of his body thrown into the sea.

A shark's digestive juices are so strong that one drop will blister a man's skin. So how could a man's arm remain undigested in a shark's stomach for so long?

At least part of the answer lies in the strange way a shark's stomach functions.

The shark does not digest its food in the stomach. Instead, the stomach is a sort of holding pen. Food—and sometimes other things like broken alarm clocks—are dumped there and held until needed. Some things may be held for days, even weeks, just how long is unknown. And what is held here may be vomited back up. In fact, many naturalists believe that sharks can vomit up the entire stomach, turning it inside out in the sea to wash, then swallowing it again. Certainly if a captured shark is lifted from the water tail first, it will often spill its stomach out of its mouth.

As its chief digestive organ, the shark uses something called the spiral valve, a part of its intestines. Enclosed in a tube, it is shaped like an auger, the bit part of a brace-and-bit, with which carpenters bore holes. As the food spirals down this, round and round, there is more time for digestive juices to act than in a straight tube.

7. *WHY DO SHARKS ATTACK HUMAN BEINGS?*

Naturalists who study sharks soon come to admire their beauty and power. They admire the perfect way sharks fit into their home element. As scavengers, sort of roving garbage trucks, the sharks are important to the ecology of the world's oceans. Some naturalists have developed a true affection for sharks.

Yet no one denies that sharks do sometimes attack, sometimes kill and eat human beings. And it is quite likely that the number of such attacks will increase. This is not because sharks will grow more vicious, but because the number of human beings who invade the home of the shark will grow. Scuba equipment was not invented until after World War II; now it is being used worldwide by an ever increasing number of divers. Snorkeling is popular wherever the water is clear. Surfing is a fast-growing sport. So, as more and more human beings invade the shark's home, there will almost certainly be a growing number of attacks.

Dr. Perry Gilbert at the Mote Marine Laboratory with the jaws of a great white shark.

THE ISLANDER

Even so, the actual number remains surprisingly small. In the early 1970s Dr. David Baldridge, a captain in the U.S. Navy, compiled a list of all the known shark attacks on human beings. He found that worldwide there were only about twenty-eight cases each year that could be proven. About 35 percent of these were fatal. As Dr. Baldridge pointed out, attacks that result in death or serious injury are far more likely to be reported than those without serious injury. Worldwide there may be many small brushes between men and sharks that are never mentioned in the newspaper. Even so, of the more than three hundred species, only thirty-five were found to be even slightly likely to attack a human.

In a book called *Shark Attack* Dr. Baldridge wrote: "Only one quarter of attack victims received wounds of a nature and number that suggest hunger provoked the attack. Sharks repeatedly attacked their victims in a wild, frenzied fashion only about 4 percent of the time."

Human beings are not part of the shark's natural prey. The shark's home is the sea and it feeds on creatures native to the sea. For most sharks, fish make up a large part of the food. Huge sharks, such as the great white, may gulp down a seal, or bite it in half. Underwater movies have shown that a person lying flat on a surfboard, paddling with his arms, will from beneath look very much like a seal. And a cruising great white may come up and take a bite. A swimmer may at times look like a fish. A frightened or wounded swimmer may thrash about in the water —and the sound will be like that of a wounded fish. Every hungry shark in the area may come rushing.

Still, only 25 percent of shark attacks appear to be caused by hunger. How about the other 75 percent?

Scientists have no absolute answer. But it is known that a shark which feels itself trapped may be a dangerous shark. Sharks, unlike some fish, cannot swim backward. They can, of course, turn right or left, but they must go headfirst. If a shark that has gone into an underwater cave finds the only exit blocked by a scuba diver, the shark may attack, not from hunger, but from fear of being trapped. Now and then a shark may enter a swash channel and find its way blocked by a sandbar or shallow water. Frightened, the shark heads back down the channel toward the open sea. If the shark thinks its escape route is blocked by a swimmer, the shark may attack. There have been a number of such cases. Usually the attack lasts only a few moments before the shark continues on its way.

Some naturalists believe that a shark will sometimes claim a

KENT CHETLAIN

The bull shark is one of the most dangerous of sharks because it frequently goes into shallow water where it may encounter human swimmers. This one was caught only a few yards off the beach.

territory as its own. This may be near a reef where food is particularly plentiful. The shark may defend its territory against a spear fisherman just as a mockingbird will defend its territory against crows and blue jays. In both cases the attack is to drive the enemy away rather than to destroy. With the shark, both can happen at the same time.

Scuba divers wearing dark wet suits have often moved freely

among schools of huge sharks without being attacked. Sometimes the sharks seem merely curious, coming close to look, then turning away. Sometimes the shark may appear more frightened than the diver. Experiments have shown that sharks often avoid dark objects or water in which a black dye has been placed. Almost certainly the diver beneath the surface, in a dark wet suit, is a bit safer than a swimmer in a bathing suit on or near the surface.

The wet suit may offer another kind of protection as well as its dark color. Both Valerie Taylor and Philippe Cousteau have told how a large shark will sometimes deliberately rub its head against the diver's wet-suited body, then turn away. Scientists believe that the shark may use its ampullae of Lorenzini, the network of pores and canals on the top of its head, just as a human being uses his tongue to taste food. If so, a light brush against the wet suit may convince the shark this is something it doesn't really want to eat.

On the other hand, if a shark brushes its sharp, toothlike scales against a swimmer's naked skin, it is very likely to bring blood. And certainly the smell of blood may excite the shark's hunger.

None of which means that a dark wet suit is absolute protection against all sharks. It is not, and wet-suited divers have been attacked.

Persons who have been attacked by sharks and who lived to tell about it almost always agree on two things. First, there is little or no physical pain in the first attack. In fact, persons have been seriously bitten without even realizing it at the moment. Probably this is because the shark's teeth are, literally, razor-sharp. Just as a man may cut himself while shaving without knowing it, so the teeth of a shark may slash through flesh and nerves so cleanly that there is at first no shock of pain.

Victims also agree on an overwhelming sense of horror, of terror, once they did realize what was happening.

This same sense of terror would be completely natural for any nearby swimmers. Despite this, some brave swimmers, both men and women, have gone to the rescue of a person being attacked. Strangely, these would-be rescuers are almost never harmed. Many shark attacks are brief, the shark striking once and going away. But even where the attack seems motivated by hunger, where the shark comes back time and again to attack, it is almost always to the original victim.

Rogue Sharks

There may be still another explanation of some shark attacks.

In India a tiger that has become lame or sick and unable to capture its natural prey will sometimes turn to human beings. Such tigers are known as rogues. And it is quite possible that there have been rogue sharks just as there have been rogue tigers. This country's most famous series of shark attacks may have been the work of a rogue great white shark.

These attacks began July 2, 1916, at Beach Haven, New Jersey. A young man named Charles VanZant was swimming not far from shore. Some witnesses said he was no more than forty feet from shore; others said he was a hundred yards away. Certainly there were a number of other swimmers nearby. Some saw a huge fin splitting the waves behind VanZant and began to shout warnings. It was too late. Screaming, VanZant disappeared under the water. At least one brave, nearby swimmer went to help. Then others. VanZant was pulled to shore. Some persons claim the shark clung to him until the water was no more than two feet deep, then turned and disappeared. Both VanZant's legs were so badly torn that he soon died from loss of blood.

Four days later a twenty-eight-year-old man named Charlie Pruder was swimming in the ocean near Spring Lake, New Jersey. This was forty-five miles up the coast from Beach Haven. Pruder was in deep water, well offshore, but a woman on the beach was watching. She called the lifeguard. "That man out there in the red canoe has turned over." What she had really seen is uncertain; probably it was the shark's body partially out of water and red with Charlie Pruder's blood. The lifeguard rowed a boat out to investigate. He found Pruder still alive, saying, "Shark! Shark bit my leg off!" Actually the lower part of both legs had been bitten off and Pruder died quickly.

That same day twenty-four persons died in New York City with polio and the papers paid little attention. But because of the human terror of sharks, Pruder's death was headline news.

There was even more terror six days later. Matawan, New Jersey, is about twenty-five miles from Spring Lake. It is not on the ocean but ten miles or so inland, on a tidal creek that does let into the Atlantic. On the morning of the twelfth of July a man standing on a bridge over the creek saw a long, dark shape pass underneath. He told about it, but no one believed a shark would be in such a small creek. That afternoon a group of boys went swimming upstream from the bridge. Twelve-year-old Lester Stilwell called to a friend, "Watch me float!" As the friend turned he saw the tail of a huge fish. An instant later Lester disappeared beneath the water. He did not resurface.

Quickly a crowd gathered. Men tried to trap the shark by stretching chicken wire across the creek. Others actually plunged into the murky water trying to locate Lester's body. One of these men was named Stanley Fisher. After one dive he came to the surface in a widening pool of blood. Men in a boat grabbed him, but Fisher died that night in a hospital.

About a half mile downstream another group of boys was

swimming. When someone shouted to them about a shark in the creek, they all swam for the bank. The last one to reach it was named Joe Dunn. He was half out of the water when the shark struck. His friends grabbed him by the arms and after a few moments the shark turned loose. Joe did not lose his life, but some of the old newspaper stories say he did lose one leg.

A few days after these attacks and less than four miles from the mouth of Matawan Creek a great white shark, eight and a half feet long, was caught in a net. In its stomach were found bits of human flesh and bones.

All these attacks had occurred with ten days. The attack of Charlie Pruder had been north of the one on VanZant; the attack on the boys had been north of that of Pruder. And all had been within an easy time-and-distance range of a great white shark. It is impossible to prove that all these attacks were the work of a single rogue shark, but there were no more attacks after the great white was killed.

8. TO KEEP SHARKS AWAY

Scientists began the serious study of sharks hoping to find a way to protect persons in the open sea from shark attack. During this study some very strange ideas were advanced.

Dr. Stewart Springer had seen a school of sharks attack and devour other wounded sharks. Yet when a shark was caught on a set line and left until it was dead, other sharks did not feed on it. They could be caught when the flesh from other fish was used for bait, but not on shark meat.

Perhaps there was something about a dead shark that drove some other sharks away.

Scientists cooked up a bar of soaplike material containing copper acetate that smelled like rotting shark. It worked beautifully—on some sharks. Unfortunately it did not seem to trouble some other species at all. At best it worked briefly—in the open sea it soon became so diluted as to have no effect.

Other studies showed that if black dye was thrown into an

1983 SEA WORLD OF FLORIDA

Both scientific researchers and professional photographers now use scuba equipment and steel cages in order to study sharks safely in their natural environment.

aquarium, sharks would avoid the dark water. But used in the open sea the dye, like the shark odor, soon washed away.

A great many other devices were tried, mostly with little success. Then C. S. Johnson at the Naval Undersea Center in California came up with an idea called the Shark Shield. It is a bag made of a strong, dark-colored plastic so thin it can be folded into a small pack. Around the top of this bag is a bright orange or yellow collar, and this collar can be blown up like a balloon. The shipwrecked sailor or downed airman can climb into the bag, then with his mouth blow up the collar. Inside the dark bag the man cannot be seen by sharks. Any body odors or blood from wounds cannot escape into the sea. And the bright collar not only keeps the bag afloat, it can be easily seen from the air.

But shark attacks are not confined to the open sea. Instead, the majority occur where people most often enter the shark's territory—along public beaches. This has been particularly true along the beaches of Australia and South Africa. Here much research has been done on how to protect an entire area from sharks.

One inventor claimed that sharks were terrified by a curtain of bubbles and would not pass through it. To curtain off a public beach with bubbles, all that was needed would be a long garden hose with holes in it, and air pumped into one end.

The invention was tested at the Lerner Marine Laboratory in the Bahamas. A bubble curtain was set up in the middle of a tank that held twelve tiger sharks. One shark swam up to the bubbles, and turned away. Even when food was placed on the other side, this shark would not pass through the curtain. But the other eleven sharks passed back and forth as if the curtain were not there. Why one shark would avoid the curtain is still unknown. But if eleven out of twelve passed casually through the bubble curtain, it would give little protection to a beach.

One inventor believed he had perfected an electrical device that would repel sharks. When Dr. Gilbert and other scientists tested it, they found it worked beautifully—on lemon sharks. Almost unbelievably, it actually attracted tiger sharks. The lemons fled; the tigers hung around as if they had found some new kind of game.

Why? Nobody knows at this time.

A different kind of electrical device has been used with success on a beach in South Africa. It is based on the principle that in an electrical field fish swim toward the positive pole. If the field is reversed, fish, including sharks, swim away. But the device was so expensive it was rarely used. However, some shrimp fishermen use a smaller and less expensive electric shield to keep sharks out of their nets.

So far the most successful method of protecting beaches has been a simple, old-fashioned way. The beach is encircled by nets. Sharks swim into the nets. They can't swim backward and so try to push through. They become entangled and die. And dead sharks help to keep at least some species of live sharks away.

9. SHARKS: HELPFUL AND SMART

Like frogs and guinea pigs, sharks have long been used in laboratories where college students are studying anatomy. These sharks are usually the spiny dogfish—a species of shark, not the ugly little fish that looks like a frog with wings and is called both dogfish and toadfish.

In the school labs, it was noticed that these spiny dogfish rarely had cancer. However, no one paid much attention to this.

When finally scientists began to study the big, man-eating sharks, they noticed the same thing. Cancer was very rare among sharks, all kinds of sharks. Cancer is fairly common in most animals, why not in sharks? And even more surprising, the scientists discovered that cancers in laboratory animals were sometimes cured by medicines made of shark-liver oil.

At the Mote Marine Laboratory in Sarasota, Florida, scientists are working to find out why. If they can learn what makes the shark immune to cancer, perhaps they can learn to prevent cancer in human beings. If so, then the shark, which has terrified people for thousands of years, will prove to be one of humanity's greatest benefactors.

How Smart Are Sharks?

As part of the study of how to prevent shark attacks, Dr. Eugenie Clark set out to learn about the shark's intelligence. It was already known that the shark had a very small brain for the size of its body. Many persons thought of it as some awesome kind of eating machine: a set of razor teeth and hungry belly that roamed the oceans, gobbling up anything alive or dead that got in the way. For this it needed only instinct. But could it learn anything new?

To find out, Dr. Eugenie Clark tested two big lemon sharks, a male and a female, at the Mote Laboratory. Working with assistants, she rigged a sixteen-inch-square target of white plywood. If this target was pushed back a few inches it would make an electrical contact and ring an underwater bell. The test was to see if the sharks could learn to ring the bell to get food.

To begin, the sharks were fed every day at exactly 3:00 P.M. directly in front of the target. Both sharks quickly learned to expect their food at this time and in this place.

Then came the first test. The target was placed in the water without food.

Instantly the male—it usually came first—rushed at the target. But when it found nothing to eat, it slowed down, then turned away, puzzled. Again it came back to the target, and again turned away. It did this several times, occasionally brushing the target lightly. Finally it hit the target hard enough to set off the underwater bell. And immediately Dr. Clark tossed it some food. The shark ate it, came back, and pushed the target again

Shark expert Dr. Eugenie Clark gives an injection to an eight-foot bull shark preparatory to a conditioning experiment.

WILLIAM M. STEPHENS

to ring the bell. Then again and again, each time getting its reward.

The female was a bit more timid than the male. But within three days both had learned to ring the bell.

Next Dr. Clark began to throw the packages of food farther and farther from the target. Each package was tied to a string so it could be pulled back after ten seconds. The sharks had to ring the bell, turn and reach the food within ten seconds or it would be taken away.

Each day Dr. Clark threw the food a little farther, always to the left. In their pen the sharks normally turned to the right, circling the pen clockwise. But if they made a right turn to reach the food it took longer and the food might be snatched away.

CAPTAIN CLYDE FORE

A lemon shark. Dr. Eugenie Clark taught two lemon sharks to ring a bell in order to obtain food.

It didn't take the sharks long to learn to turn left.

In fact, the male shark, which usually fed first, would sometimes ring the bell, then swim aside to let the female feed. But just why, Dr. Clark did not know.

Finally Dr. Clark tried an experiment that had tragic results. It had already been proved that sharks had much better eyesight than was once thought. But were they color blind? Most naturalists thought so.

Dr. Clark painted the white target yellow and placed it in the water at feeding time. As usual the male came rushing toward it. But two feet away it slammed on the brakes by lowering its pectoral fins. It not only stopped, it did a back flip, coming completely out of the water. It began to swim wildly, first in one direction then another. The female, too, began to swim wildly, the two banging together time after time.

In a few days the female was once more acting normally. But not the male. It would not go near the target whether it was white or yellow. It refused all food. As it starved it swam more slowly. It kept its head turned to one side, its body twisted. Dr. Clark wondered if it had hurt its back in the wild leap after it first saw the yellow target. There were times, however, when it did straighten its body briefly and swim normally.

Whatever the reason, the male died two months after it confronted the yellow target. The reasons for its strange behavior are still not understood.

10. SHARKS AND PORPOISES

Many persons believe that sharks and bottle-nosed dolphins, *Tursiops truncatus*, commonly called porpoises, are born enemies. They have been called "the dogs and cats of the sea." Many fishermen have seen battles between sharks and porpoises. In most of these accounts the porpoise wins by fiercely butting its head against the shark. On the other hand, porpoise flesh has been found in the stomach of sharks.

But are they natural enemies? Naval officers began to wonder if a porpoise could be trained to guard deep-sea divers against possible shark attacks. They asked Mote Laboratory scientists to study the matter.

The laboratory people captured an eight-foot porpoise in the Gulf of Mexico and put it in a large circular pool. They named it Simo, the Greek word for "snub-nosed." After it had been in the pool long enough to feel at home, they brought in a shark about Simo's size

Simo and the shark eyed one another. Simo made a few clicking noises, but that was all. Shark and porpoise were not friendly, but neither did they fight.

Another shark of a different species was added to the pool, then a third shark. Simo paid little heed to them, or the sharks to him.

The sharks were removed from the pool and tests started to see if Simo could be trained to attack sharks. A dead shark was placed in the water and the trainer held Simo's food close to it. When Simo took the food it rang an underwater bell. Simo quickly learned the bell meant food, and the place to get it was beside the dead shark. Then the trainer put his hand in the water, close to the shark, but without food. Only when Simo butted his head against the shark did he get food. And the harder he butted the more food he got.

A large, live sandbar shark was placed in the pool. Simo ignored it until the bell was rung. That meant food and the way to get it was to butt the shark. Simo did, and the shark fled through the gate into an adjoining pool.

Next a nurse shark was brought into the pool, then a large lemon shark. On signal, Simo battered each of them and sent them rushing to the safety of the adjoining tank.

Now a bull shark was placed in the pool and the signal given to attack. Simo not only didn't attack, he went swimming crazily around the tank making clicking and squalling noises. Meanwhile, the bull shark ignored him.

It took five days to calm Simo down, and he never did attack the bull shark. The bull shark, *Carcharhinus leucas*, is one of the most dangerous to human beings. It is also—and here is a thing that puzzled the Mote scientists—almost identical to the sandbar shark. It is practically impossible to tell them apart. But Simo attacked the sandbar shark without hesitation, and almost went crazy when confronted with the bull shark.

Nobody ever found out just why. Money for the experiment gave out, and Simo was returned to the open gulf.

The tests at Mote Laboratory and others at the Lerner Marine Laboratory in Bimini showed that sharks and porpoises are not natural enemies. When both were well fed they got along together. Yet they have been seen fighting in the open sea.

Thomas Helm, in a book called *Shark, Unpredictable Killer of the Sea*, tells of watching one such battle.

Helm and a friend were fishing in shallow water just off the west coast of Florida. Nearby, a huge hammerhead shark leaped half out of the water and fell back with a tremendous splash.

One thousand lemon sharks were caught, measured, marked, injected with tetracycline and released for Dr. Sam Gruber's study of the role of the lemon shark as a predator in the tropical marine environment. Dr. Gruber studies sharks at the University of Miami.

S. SPIELMAN

Around it Helm saw a swarm of shadows and the dorsal fins of many porpoises. While the fishermen watched, the porpoises circled the shark. Then, suddenly, one porpoise would rush the shark, slam head-on into it, and whirl away. The big hammerhead tried to face each attacker, but there were too many porpoises and they were too fast. Probably the shark did bite some; the fishermen saw blood in the water and the tail of one porpoise, waving above the surface, was torn into shreds.

Gradually the hammerhead's movements became slower. The battering rams of the porpoises continued. At last the shark, motionless, sank slowly to the bottom. The porpoises swam away.

Helm thought that perhaps the fight started with the porpoises defending their young. But he could not be certain.

Dr. Stewart Springer saw a different type of shark-porpoise battle. He was on a research ship in the Gulf of Mexico, moving slowly, when a band of about fifty porpoises came alongside. Porpoises often play about the bows of ships, but these behaved strangely. Watching closely, Springer saw that in the band were about eight very young porpoises, no more than three feet long. These were pushed in close against the ship. Just outside of them were middle-sized porpoises. And beyond these, on the outer edge of the half circle, swam a half dozen or so of the biggest porpoises.

All of them, young and old, swam slowly, as if totally exhausted. A number of the bigger porpoises were newly wounded.

About fifty yards away Dr. Springer saw the dorsal fins and shadowy outlines of a huge school of sharks. While he watched, one giant shark left the school and came rushing toward the porpoises. The big porpoises in the outer ring whirled to meet it. The action was underwater and too fast for Springer to follow exactly: There was a great splashing, boiling water—and the giant shark turned away. The porpoises returned to their positions. They were using the ship to protect their band on one side.

The sharks far outnumbered the porpoises. Many of them were much bigger. If they had attacked as a group they could have destroyed the porpoises. Certainly they could have killed and eaten the young. But each shark attacked alone. The porpoises worked together.

The ship's crew wanted to help the porpoises. But how? They tried dropping food over the side, but the porpoises seemed too tired to eat.

For half an hour the sharks attacked, one at a time. Each shark was met by a group of porpoises and beaten back.

A sudden summer squall struck the research vessel. The rain was so hard it was impossible to see more than a few feet. It lasted perhaps a half hour. Then the rain quit, the sun came out, and both the porpoises and sharks had disappeared. Dr. Springer felt sure the porpoises had taken advantage of the weather to escape.

In captivity the shark and the porpoise do not appear to be natural enemies, the dog and cat of the sea. On the other hand, in the open sea a hungry shark will certainly feed on a smaller porpoise—if it can. The porpoise does not have the shark's razor-like teeth, but it is faster, more intelligent, and no easy prey.

11. SHARK FISHING, FOR SPORT

Sport fishermen once considered the shark as no more than a nuisance. Persons who would spend a fortune trying to catch a marlin or a broadbill swordfish would merely grunt in disgust at the mention of shark. The shark was considered a slow, sluggish fish that put up very little fight for its size.

This is true of some species of sharks, but far from true of others. In recent years more and more sport fishermen have come to recognize this. Shark fishing has become tremendously popular wherever salt-water fishermen gather. There are shark fishing clubs all along the coastal waters of the United States, Australia, South Africa, wherever the shark is plentiful.

The International Game Fish Association now recognizes a number of species of sharks as game fish. And since these sharks are often too big to be taken out of the water and weighed on anything but the biggest of scales, there is an accepted formula for estimating the weight. This is written:

$$\frac{\text{Girth}^2 \times \text{length}}{800} = \text{weight.}$$

That is, measure the distance around the shark's belly in inches. Multiply this figure by itself. Multiply the result by the length of the shark in inches and divide the total by eight hundred.

Many shark fishermen consider the mako as the greatest game fish of them all. The average mako will be about six to eight feet long and weigh around two hundred pounds. A truly big one may be over twelve feet and weigh more than a thousand pounds. But it is not its size that makes the mako a great game fish. Hooked, it may jump twenty feet out of the water, time after time. Zane Grey, a great fisherman as well as a writer of Western novels, told of seeing a five-hundred-pound mako jump six times, ". . . the second higher than the first, the third highest, and nearly thirty feet, the remaining three graduating down. This shark turned over twice in the air at the top of his jump."

G. B. KNOWLES

The blacktip shark is much prized by sport fishermen because when hooked it will leap out of the water and spin about. In fact, it will sometimes do this, apparently for fun, or perhaps to shake itself free of parasites, without being hooked.

The mako, Grey said, had a mouth that looked like a subway entrance with spiked gates. It is a good description. The mako's teeth are almost as long as a man's fingers and curved like a tiger's claws. They are not only needle-pointed, but razor-sharp along both edges.

If danger is an important element of excitement, then certainly the mako is one of the most exciting game fish. It will not only jump and fight furiously for its freedom, it may turn and attack the boat from which it has been hooked. And a mako's teeth can take huge chunks from a wooden hull. More than one mako has actually turned hunter rather than hunted, jumping inside the fishing boat, smashing chairs, splintering the deck, and not killing the fisherman simply because the mako could not follow him onto the bow or atop the cabin.

Peter Goadby who has written about fishing around the world has told about one mako that he *almost* caught. It probably weighed about one thousand pounds. Probably, because it was never weighed. After a long fight the mako was brought alongside the boat. It looked to be completely exhausted, almost dead. With gloved hands Goadby caught the leader wire and lifted the huge shark's head above the surface. Crewmen sank two flying gaffs into the head, one on each side of the jaw.

Without warning the mako exploded from the water, straight up, higher than the heads of the men on the boat. Goadby still had the leader around his gloved hands and the leap of the fish took him with it "like a two-hundred-pound live cork from a champagne bottle," as he later wrote.

Fortunately this mako did not turn to fight the boat or to look for Goadby in the water. Its leap tore one gaff free. A moment later its rush snapped the rope to the other gaff, and it was gone. Peter Goadby, climbing back into his boat, was glad to have seen the last of it.

Shark Fishing—for Money

In some parts of the world shark fishing has always been an important business because shark meat was an important part of the people's food. Shark meat, well cooked, can be very tasty, yet it has never been popular in the United States.

There are several reasons for this. Many persons think of sharks as man-eaters, so eating shark might seem to be a form of cannibalism. More important, probably, is that a shark, to be eaten, must be cleaned very soon after it is caught. Otherwise the flesh breaks down and gives off a strong smell of ammonia. Anyone who gets a whiff of this doesn't want anything to do with the meat. So many persons came to believe that sharks always smelled like this and never learned better.

In Japan and China, especially, many excellent dishes are made from shark meat. A delicious, and expensive, soup made from shark fins is sold in Chinese restaurants around the world. In England and Australia "fish 'n chips" is about as popular as hot dogs in America. And the fish is very likely to be shark.

Shark fishing as a business reached its peak in the United States during World War II. Until that time the main source of vitamin A was cod-liver oil. Most of this came from Europe and with the war going on, it was difficult to get. Then it was dis-

These are shark fins being dried for shipment to restaurants where they will be made into an expensive shark fin soup.

FLORIDA DEPARTMENT OF NATURAL RESOURCES

FLORIDA DEPARTMENT OF NATURAL RESOURCES

A shark hide with the scales removed is being dried and tanned for leather.

covered that oil from the liver of a spiny dogfish shark contained about ten times as much vitamin A as cod-liver oil. All along the coasts of the United States shark fishing became an important business.

But vitamins were not the only thing that could be obtained from sharks. Remember that a shark's scales are actually tiny teeth. The shark's skin made an excellent fine sandpaper. If the scales were removed and the skin tanned, it made a very strong, handsome, and expensive leather. Sharks' teeth were frequently made into jewelry.

Most of the fishermen who caught sharks for money did so by long-lining. That is exactly what it sounds like. A long line—

some of them were as much as twenty-five miles long, though most were much shorter—was used. In the open sea each end was attached to a float, with other floats at various places along the line. From this long line hung shorter lines, and to these were attached baited hooks. A hooked shark, no matter how powerful, had the weight of the line and floats to fight against. There might be other hooked sharks pulling in other directions. Eventually the shark dies.

If the long line was used in an area frequently crossed by ships, it was fastened to the bottom by weights. Floats at each end made it possible for the fisherman to find it again.

Fishermen who worked on a smaller scale might use only one or two short lines, with one end of each line fastened to the boat. But this could be dangerous, if the line was so strong and the shark so big it might sink the boat.

During the war the price of shark-liver oil rose to thirteen dollars a pound, and fishermen were bringing in as much as 9 million tons a year. But in 1950 scientists learned to make vitamin A in the laboratory. Prices dropped. Also, sharks reproduce slowly compared to most fishes. Heavily fished in one area, the shark population would sink to where fishing was no longer profitable. Now there are very few commercial shark fisheries in the United States.

12. SHARK LEGENDS

For thousands of years people have been afraid of sharks, and this fear has inspired talk. When little is truly known about a subject, almost any story can be believed.

As mentioned, many people still think a shark must turn upside down to bite. The location of the shark's mouth underneath the head makes this easy to believe—if you did not know the shark's upper jaw can move as well as the lower one.

Why many persons believe that a shark will not attack in shallow water is something of a mystery. Actually, many of the confirmed attacks have been in water less than shoulder deep.

In the days of sailing ships many sailors believed that if a person died on the ship, a blue shark would quickly begin to follow. And it would keep following until the dead person was buried at sea. Whereupon the shark had a meal.

To carry that superstition further, many sailors believed that if a blue shark began to follow a ship, it was a sure sign someone would die before the voyage was over.

On the tropical islands of the Pacific the natives live in close contact with the sea. And it is here the shark legends grow most wild and wonderful. Strangely, in many of these stories the shark is not always evil but often a god capable of both good and evil.

In one of the Hawaiian legends the king of the sharks is named Kama-Hoa-Lii, and he spent much of his time helping out Hawaiians lost at sea. If prayed to, he might guide them back to their island himself; more likely he would send one of his servant sharks to act as guide. Sometimes Kama-Hoa-Lii would appear alongside a boat that was about to sink in a storm. The waters would grow calm and the boat would make it safely back to land.

But there was also another side to Kama-Hoa-Lii. At will he could change himself into a very handsome young man. Then he would go ashore to make love to the island's most beautiful girls. If a child was born of this it was always a boy, human in every way except that across his back was a mark like that of a shark's mouth. And such a boy must never be allowed to eat meat. If he did, he would follow other natives to the beach, slip into the water behind them, turn into a shark and eat the people who had been his friends a few minutes before.

In another Hawaiian legend, the kings staged duels between sharks and male swimmers. For these duels, sharks were lured into a shallow lagoon. There they were kept until half starved. Then a man went into the water armed with a knife made from a piece of wood with a shark's tooth fastened to it. When the hungry shark attacked, the man tried to dive beneath it and rip open the shark's belly.

According to the legend, the shark won most of the fights, but not all.

One of the strangest shark legends is about Lake Nicaragua. This is a freshwater lake in Nicaragua. It is surrounded by mountains, and how the sharks got here is uncertain. But there they are, many of them, and—according to the story anyway—they never attacked a living person. The natives in turn never fished for or harmed the sharks. But when a person died, he or she was dressed in the best clothing and jewelry, and fed to the sharks. This had been going on for several hundred years when a greedy outsider heard the story. Secretly he began to catch the sharks and open them up to recover the jewelry. Unfortunately, for him, the natives caught him at it—and fed him to the sharks.

Or so the story goes.

13. PREDICTABLE, OR UNPREDICTABLE?

Professional divers, scientists, photographers, men and women who dive for sport have spent hours swimming among sharks, sometimes touching them, actually feeding them, without harm. Other divers, as well as children playing in shallow water, have been attacked and killed.

How predictable is the shark? Why does it sometimes attack a human being, and sometimes turn and race away as if terrified? Even the people who have spent years studying sharks do not agree. Indeed, their opinions of sharks may differ from hate and loathing to downright affection.

When Zane Grey saw a giant tiger shark he had caught hauled dead out of the water he shouted, "Well, Mr. Man-eater, you will never kill any boy or girl!" He felt, he wrote, "a deep and powerful emotion—passion and primal exultance."

But in a book called *Great Shark Stories*, Valerie Taylor, the Australian diver and photographer, wrote, "I find it sad that

THE ISLANDER

A tiger shark, right foreground.

Grey could look upon his dead tiger shark, that had fought so long and hard for its life, and see it as a vicious brute . . . We have always found tiger sharks, in their natural element, even when feeding, to be rather placid in nature."

Mrs. Taylor has probably spent as much time diving among sharks as anyone anywhere. Once, wearing a suit of specially designed armor, she deliberately put her arm in a shark's mouth —and escaped with only minor injury. She sincerely believes that all sharks are far less dangerous than most persons think. In Australia the gray nurse shark is thought to be one of the most dangerous. Valerie Taylor—without any armor—swam into an underwater cave with thirteen gray nurse sharks. They were young, about one year old, and "only" six feet long. They did not harm her. "Poor little babies," she wrote later, "all they wanted was to be left in peace."

Not many persons can feel as sympathetic toward all sharks as Valerie Taylor. However, most scientists do believe that the shark is not quite so dangerous as commonly thought. One wrote that the majority of shark bites actually occurred after the shark had been caught and pulled onto a dock or the deck of a boat. In one instance a diver used his knife to prop open the mouth of a shark that had been speared and believed dead. Then he knelt and put his hand in the shark's mouth to have his photograph taken. The shark twitched, the knife slipped, and the shark's jaws slashed through the fisherman's hand. But the newspapers reported that the diver had been "mauled" by the shark.

Dr. Eugenie Clark believes that the shark is unpredictable because we do not yet know enough about it. The more we learn —and there is still a vast amount to be learned—the better we will be able to understand how and why a shark will act.

14. WHAT TO DO WHEN YOU SEE A SHARK

The Office of Naval Research once asked the Shark Research Panel of the American Institute of Biological Sciences for advice on how swimmers should act if confronted by a shark. The answer came in three sections: To Swimmers and Bathers, To Skin and Scuba Divers, To Survivors of Air and Sea Disasters.

To Swimmers and Bathers: The first advice is get out of the water, and get out as quickly and quietly as possible. Don't panic. Don't thrash about trying to swim faster than you have ever swum before. Remember that sharks are attracted by the sounds of struggle. Swim with a steady, rhythmic beat.

Don't swim alone. Swim with a buddy or in a group. Sharks more often attack a lone swimmer than one in a crowd.

If dangerous sharks are known to be in the area, don't go swimming.

Blood attracts sharks, so if you have an open wound or sore, don't go in the water.

Don't swim in water that is very rough or dirty. If the underwater visibility is poor, you may not see the shark, but the shark may sense your vibrations.

To Skin and Scuba Divers: Don't dive alone. Use the buddy system. Always have a companion.

Do not spear a shark. Even a small shark when injured may turn on what it believes has injured it. The vibrations of a wounded shark, as well as its blood, may attract other sharks, including big ones.

Don't try to hitch a ride on a shark's tail or dorsal fin. The shark might simply try to escape; it might also turn and bite.

Don't swim around towing a string of speared fish. Get each fish out of the water promptly.

As a rule, a shark will circle its intended victim several times before attacking. If a shark begins to circle you, get out of the water as quickly as possible, but swim with a steady beat. If wearing scuba, remain under the surface. If the shark moves in before you can reach your boat, turn to face it. (Valerie Taylor believes that if a shark comes close, a swimmer should turn to face it even without scuba or snorkel. Sharks, she says, don't like to be looked at. Surfers should paint two big eyes on the underwater side of their surfboards.) Divers likely to encounter sharks should carry a short, heavy club. A blow on the nose with a "shark billy" will often drive a shark away. However, a blow with the fist against the shark's rough hide may cut your hand and bring blood. Simply blowing bubbles or shouting underwater will sometimes send a shark fleeing.

To Survivors of Air and Sea Disasters: Don't take off your clothing in the water. Clothing, especially on the feet and legs, is your only protection against the rough skin of a passing shark.

Wounded survivors, anyone bleeding, should be placed in a raft, out of the water. In fact, everyone should be in the raft if there is room.

If you must swim, do so with a regular, steady beat.

Don't throw blood or garbage out of the raft since it may attract sharks.

Don't fish from a raft if sharks are nearby. If a fish is hooked and sharks come after it, let them have it, quickly.

If a group of persons in the water is threatened by sharks, form a circle facing outward. If a shark comes close, hit it on the snout with any available object other than the human hand. Use that as a last resort.

15. THE MAN-EATERS

THE GREAT WHITE SHARK, *Carcharodon carcharias*,
FAMILY LAMNIDAE OR MACKERAL SHARKS

Carcharodon carcharias goes by many names: white shark, great white shark, white death, white pointer, man-eater, and others. Under any name it is the most awesome, the most fearful, and the most feared of all sharks. It is the subject of the wildest shark stories, the shark most often said to devour boats as well as people.

Actually, there are several species that more frequently do harm to human beings than does the great white. This is not because the great white is less than truly fearful, but because it is quite rare.

The range of the great white is tremendous. It is found—sometimes—in practically all tropical to temperate waters. Off the United States it roams the Atlantic from Newfoundland to Florida. It has been found in the Gulf of Mexico, and in the

GORDON WHITNEY, THE ISLANDER

This great white shark, estimated to be about nineteen to twenty feet in length, was caught by a commercial fisherman on set line in the Gulf of Mexico near Anna Maria Island in 1937. Here it is being hauled onto the beach by a rope attached to a truck.

Pacific from Alaska to Mexico. But nowhere is it found very often. Sport fishermen have spent small fortunes trying to catch a great white shark without ever seeing, no less catching one. Jacques-Yves Cousteau, whose life has been devoted to diving all over the world, has seen only two great white sharks—and both of these turned and fled as if they were more afraid of him than he was of them!

That, of course, is not the usual behavior of the great white. They have been known to attack fishing boats, probably thinking the boat was some kind of fish. They have killed and eaten people. One that was caught by a sports fisherman was found to have an entire horse in its stomach. Another contained a seven-foot shark.

It is often claimed that the great white may get to be forty feet long, but there is no scientific proof of this. The biggest ever measured was caught off the coast of Cuba in 1941. It was twenty-one feet long and probably weighed around five thousand pounds. "Probably" because there were no scales strong enough to weigh it.

An eighteen-foot great white for which there were scales weighed 4,150 pounds. Its liver alone weighed almost six hundred pounds. When the jaws were propped open, they measured two feet, three inches from top to bottom and one foot, ten inches from side to side. The teeth were over two inches long, triangular in shape. Their edges were serrated like the blade of a saw and, literally, razor-sharp.

The great white shark isn't really white. Its back is more likely to be gray or even brown turning into a dirty white on the belly. The first dorsal fin is high, the second dorsal very small.

No great white shark has been kept alive in captivity for very long and little is known about their reproductive system. They are believed to be ovoviviparous—that is, the female's eggs hatch inside the mother and the young feed on the egg yolk, or sometimes on unfertilized eggs or on other, smaller young. They are probably about four feet long at birth, but the smallest, free-swimming great white ever caught was fifty-one inches long and weighed thirty-six pounds.

The Requiem Sharks, Family Carcharhinidae, Oceanic White-tipped, Bull, Tiger

The great white shark gets the most publicity as a man-eater. But Jacques-Yves Cousteau once wrote that the oceanic white-tipped shark, *Carcharhinus longimanus*, is "the only species of shark that is never frightened by the approach of a diver, and they are the most dangerous of all sharks." The oceanic white-

CAPTAIN CLYDE FORE

The bull shark. It frequently goes into shallow water where swimmers may be found. It even goes in and out of freshwater. This often brings it into contact with human beings—and so it probably is responsible for more attacks on people than any other species of shark.

tipped shark, however, keeps to the open seas, as its name implies. It is never found around swimming beaches, and so is rarely seen. It is the bull shark, *Carcharhinus leucas*, a close relative of the white-tipped, that is probably responsible for more attacks on human beings than any other species of shark.

The bull shark, unlike the great white, is plentiful. It can be found almost anywhere the water is warm. In North America it is common from New York south, around Florida and through the Gulf of Mexico. On the West Coast it is found most often off southern California, and only rarely goes north. Where it does go, unlike the white-tipped shark, is into shallow water. And not only into shallow water, but into freshwater. It has been found a thousand miles up the Mississippi River, before the building of dams and locks blocked its way. It has attacked human beings in the Ganges River in India and the Tigres in Iraq. It is the bull shark that lives in Lake Nicaragua in Central America. And it is this custom of feeding in the same waters where people frequently go swimming that makes it most dangerous.

Reproduction in the bull shark is viviparous, like mammals. Young bull sharks are often found in shallow bays and near the mouths of rivers. Here the water is less salty than in the open sea. Perhaps the females come here to bear their young. And this may be the reason the adult bull shark can move from salt water into fresh and back again without trouble. There is a great deal still to be learned about *Carcharhinus leucas.*

The bull shark gets its common name from its "bull-headed" look. The snout is very short; actually its mouth from corner to corner is wider than the snout is long. The first dorsal fin is high with a pointed tip, the second dorsal much smaller. The teeth are triangular and saw-edged. In color the bull shark runs from a pale to dark gray on the back, white on the belly. The fins are black-tipped when young, but this fades as the shark matures. As with many sharks, the females are usually bigger than the males. The average male will be about seven feet long and weigh about two hundred pounds. Females may be over eleven feet and weigh five hundred pounds.

Both the bull and the oceanic white-tipped shark belong to the scientific family Carcharhinidae, usually called the requiem

G. B. KNOWLES, THE ISLANDER

Shark jaws make frightening decorations. These are the jaws of a tiger shark.

sharks. It is one of the largest shark families with more than twenty species found near the United States. Not all of them can be called man-eaters, but certainly the tiger shark, *Galeocerdo cuvieri*, should be listed with the bulls and the oceanic white-tippeds as dangerous.

The tiger shark gets its name from its looks, and it is one of the easiest species to recognize. The back is dark; it may be almost black or a dark bluish-green. The underside may be white or yellowish. The first dorsal fin is much higher than the second. The caudal fin is very long and pointed. Behind the eye is a small but visible spiracle. (The spiracle is a gill slit that provides oxygen for blood that flows directly to the shark's eyes and brain through a separate blood vessel. Not all sharks have this.) But it is the tiger markings that make it easy to recognize. The young tiger shark might almost be called leopard, since its back and sides are spotted rather than striped. But as the shark matures the spots grow together to form stripes much like those of its jungle namesake.

Normally tiger sharks feed on such things as stingrays, crabs, clams, turtles, and other fish. But they seem willing to gulp down almost anything that gets in the way. It was a tiger shark that was found to contain part of a crocodile, a sheep, three sea gulls, and two unopened cans of peas. The stomach of another held three overcoats and a raincoat. Just how it managed to get this collection is unknown. Inside another tiger shark was a whole chicken coop with feathers and bones.

The tiger shark, which may get to be fourteen feet long or even bigger, often feeds on smaller sharks. But this is not a trait of the tiger alone. Dr. Stewart Springer was doing research on sharks near the mouth of the Mississippi River when he caught a large tiger shark. In its stomach he found a bull shark. In the bull shark's stomach he found a black-tip shark. And in the stomach of the black-tip was a dogfish shark. Dr. Springer claimed a record for the most sharks on a single hook.

Unfortunately, the tiger shark has also been known to feed on human beings. In theWest Indies it is one of the most feared of all species. And yet scuba divers have often seen tiger sharks, sometimes large numbers of them, that ignored the divers completely.

CAPTAIN CLYDE FORE

This is the dusky shark, a member of the requiem shark family. Like most members of that family, it may be dangerous to man.

Hammerhead Sharks, Family Sphyrnidae

There are nine species of hammerhead sharks. The little bonnethead, *Syhyrna tiburo*, rarely gets to be more than three or three and a half feet long. *Sphyrna corona*, which doesn't seem to have a common name, is even smaller. But then there is the great hammerhead, *Sphyrna mokarran*, that will frequently grow to fourteen feet and maybe to twenty feet. The other species fall in between, and, except for size, they all look much alike.

The great hammerhead is the chief reason for listing this family as possible man-eaters. But even the little bonnet shark has been known to turn and bite a diver stupid enough to grab it by the tail.

You have only to look at a hammerhead shark to know why it is called that. But why this family has developed such a strangely shaped head is uncertain. There are, however, several possible benefits.

The hammerhead has an eye and a nostril at each end of its

This is a seventeen-foot, one-inch great hammerhead caught in the Gulf of Mexico.

THE ISLANDER

ROBERT PRESNAL, BEACH CAMERA

The teeth of a great hammerhead.

head. In a big hammerhead these may be as much as three feet apart. And, even more than most sharks, the hammerhead swings its head from side to side while swimming. If it is hunting its food by smell, it may pick up the odor first in one nostril, then the other. This way it might be able to home in on its prey more accurately than otherwise. And the same way with its eyes.

The ampullae of Lorenzini, the network of canals and ducts that not only helps a shark sense vibrations in the water but also electrical impulses, is spread all across the hammerhead's wide head. This may increase its sensitivity to electrical fields. No one knows for sure. But we do know that the stingray is one of the hammerhead's favorite foods. And stingrays often bury themselves in the sand. Lying still, they cause no sound vibrations in the water. They do, however, like all living creatures, create a small electrical field. And hammerheads find them, no matter how still they lie.

It is true that other sharks also find buried and motionless rays. But to judge from their stomach contents, the hammerhead is the champion ray eater. One great hammerhead had ninety-six stingray barbs stuck in its mouth, jaws, and even on the outside of its head. This didn't seem to bother the hammerhead.

Hammerheads are viviparous. The pups vary in size and number by species, much as they will later in life. Bonnet sharks usually have eight to twelve pups at a time, each about twelve inches long. The great hammerhead may have twenty to forty pups, each slightly over two feet long.

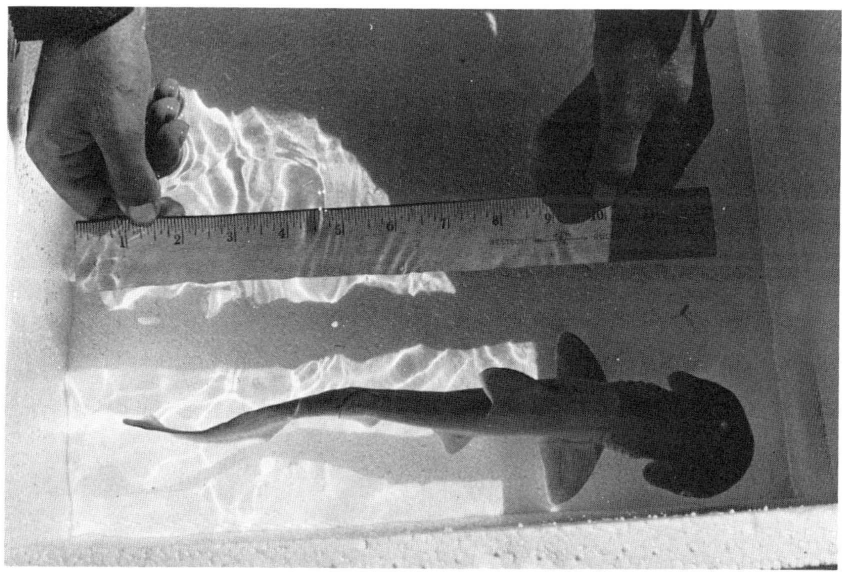

1983 SEA WORLD OF FLORIDA

The bonnethead shark is also called the shovelhead, and gets its name from the shape of the head.

These are not the only species of sharks that may be dangerous to man. At least thirty-five species, including the mako and the blue shark, have been known to attack human beings. In fact, almost any shark may be dangerous under certain circumstances. Even the placid basking shark might accidentally swat a swimmer with its tail. Or jump clear of the water trying to get rid of parasites, and comes down on a human being. But certainly the great white, some of the requiem sharks, and the great hammerhead are among the most dangerous in American waters.

16. HUGE AND HARMLESS

The Basking Shark, *Cetorhinus maximus*, Family Cetorhinidae

The basking shark needs to have its Latin name changed. *Cetorhinus maximus* means biggest whale shark: *Cetos* is whale and *rhiny* is shark. *Maximus* is where we get the English word maximum, the biggest possible. But actually there is another shark, *Rhincodon typus*, called the whale shark, even bigger than *Cetorhinus maximus*.

There is even some doubt about its common name, basking shark. True, it is often seen swimming very slowly just beneath the surface with both the first dorsal and the tip of the caudal fin showing. It appears to be simply basking in the sunlight. But it is probably much more interested in feeding than in basking.

No matter what the name, the basking shark is a very curious and interesting creature.

It may not be the biggest of all fish, but it is next to the biggest. Just an average-size basking shark will be somewhere between twenty-two and thirty feet long. You couldn't get it through the door of the average home, and if you did you couldn't jam it into the average living room. This average basking shark would weigh around eight thousand pounds. Of course, there are bigger ones. Some persons claim to have seen basking sharks that would measure forty-five feet—had there been any way to measure them. On the other hand, this may well be an exaggeration.

Even the babies are big. Very little is yet known about the reproduction of the basking shark. They are believed to be live bearers, either viviparous or ovoviparous. The smallest basking shark on record was sixty-five inches long, and they are probably that big at birth.

Most sharks are famous, or infamous, for the size and number of their teeth. The basking shark has teeth all right, a hundred or more to the row, and row upon row. But they are tiny and play little or no part in the shark's feeding. The basking shark feeds entirely upon plankton. Plankton in Greek means "wandering," and in English it refers to all the tiny plant and animal life of the ocean that, on the whole, is too small to move itself and "wanders" with the tides and currents. Much of it is too small to be seen with the naked eye. Much is made up of copepods, tiny animals kin to lobsters and shrimp, barely visible. Scientists figure that it takes about a thousand pounds of copepods to make one hundred pounds of the fish that eats them. And it is this on which the eight-thousand-pound basking shark feeds.

To catch its plankton, the basking shark swims slowly with its mouth open. It is a big mouth, even for a shark. Back of the mouth are the gill slits, and these are enormous. They extend from high on the back almost to the middle of the throat—almost all the way around the basking shark's head. Inside the gills are

© CHUCK DAVIS PHOTO

An approximately twenty-foot-long basking shark feeds just below the ocean's surface off the coast of Southern California. The shark was photographed in the Santa Barbara Channel, several miles off the shore of Santa Barbara.

the gill rakers. These are bristlelike fibers that have a sticky coating. As the basking shark swims, water enters its open mouth, passes over the gill rakers, and out the gill slits. The gills take oxygen from the water. Drifting plankton collects on the sticky gill rakers. Now and then the basking shark will close its mouth, tighten its gills, and swallow the plankton from off its gill rakers.

Fortunately for the basking shark, the seas in which it spends most of its time are rich in plankton. And scientists figure that an average-size basking shark, swimming at two knots, can filter a thousand tons of seawater over its gills every hour.

The basking shark likes colder water than do most sharks. Off North America it ranges from Newfoundland to North Carolina, very rarely going as far south as Florida. In the Pacific it is common from the Gulf of Alaska to Baja, California.

The liver of an average basking shark will produce as much as two hundred gallons of oil, and so for many years it was hunted off the coasts of Ireland, Scotland, and Norway. But only in the summer. In the winter the basking shark simply disappeared. Where it went, nobody knew.

Now and then bodies of basking sharks would wash up on an Irish or Scottish beach during the winter. And when scientists examined these bodies they found that the gill rakers had disappeared. How then did they eat?

Naturalists are still trying to learn. Some believe that during the winter the basking shark goes into very deep water and semihibernates. At this time it would need very little food while it grew new gill rakers. Another theory is that after losing its gill rakers, the basking shark dives to the bottom of the sea and feeds on the plants and small shellfish it finds there.

Neither idea would explain another mystery of the basking shark. In the Atlantic they disappear during the winter; off California the sharks are present the year round. In fact, during the winter they are fairly common. It is during the summer they become rare. But where they go is unknown.

Basking sharks have played a part in still another mystery of the sea. They frequently go in schools. At times they seem to play follow-the-leader, going in long lines, one close behind the other, sometimes so close that the nose of one shark will rub against the tail of another. Sometimes they form huge circles, going round and round. Seen from a slight distance, the slow rise and fall of dorsal and caudal fins, the humped backs, they may appear to be one gigantic animal. No doubt many a sailor has stared in awe at what he believed to be some monstrous sea serpent.

WHALE SHARK, *Rhincodon typus*, FAMILY RHINCODONTIDAE

The whale shark is the biggest fish in the sea. Some true whales are bigger, but whales are mammals. Just how big the whale shark can get is uncertain. A whale shark thirty-nine feet long has been captured and measured, but some that appear to be much bigger have been seen. It is quite possible that some whale sharks grow to be forty-five feet long and weigh around thirty thousand pounds. That's the same weight as 150 men if each weighed two hundred pounds.

The whale shark would be easy to identify even if it were not so huge. The back is reddish gray, the belly white. All across its back, even across the head and tail and dorsal fins, there are white or yellowish spots. On the back these spots run up and down between yellow-white stripes. Along each side from head to tail are three strong ridges. These merge into the caudal keel near the tail.

The whale shark's mouth is much closer to the tip of the snout than that of most sharks. It has teeth, hundreds and hundreds

Whale shark.

of them, but they are not much bigger than those of the basking shark. Like the basking shark, the whale shark may feed by slowly swimming along, its mouth open, its gill rakers straining plankton from the water. But the whale shark may also eat some larger items such as shellfish, squid, and even fairly big fish at times.

The whale shark is not known to swim in family circles like the basking shark, but it does have a trick of its own. It has often been seen bobbing up and down in the water, head up, tail down, coming high out of the water and sinking again. It does this with its mouth open, and apparently swallows any fish it happens to catch on the way up.

The whale shark likes warmer water than its basking relative. It is found in all tropical seas, but usually far offshore. So not many divers are apt to meet up with it. When they do, the only danger is being accidentally swatted by its tail. The whale shark is a gentle giant. Some professional divers who have met the whale shark have also taken rides holding to its dorsal fin. It was, said one, like clinging to an underwater freight train.

INDEX